The
Better Allies™
Approach
to Hiring

KAREN CATLIN

Better Allies Press

ALSO BY KAREN CATLIN

Better Allies:
Everyday Actions to Create Inclusive, Engaging Workplaces

Present! A Techie's Guide to Public Speaking
(coauthored with Poornima Vijayashanker)

CONTENTS

INTRODUCTION

Companies will enter the new year amid a labor shortage so acute that any downturn in the economy isn't likely to put much of a dent in it. With more than seven million jobs unfilled, employers have been piling on free snacks, comfortable lounges and cafes and other perks to burnish their image in the job market.

They're going to have to go deeper. What will distinguish the most profitable companies from the rest in the coming year won't be whether they offer foosball or free food. It will be whether leaders foster a workplace culture where employees feel a sense of belonging, like their jobs and trust their managers to help them move on to a better one.

—Sue Shellenbarger, "Why Perks No Longer Cut It for Workers," *Wall Street Journal,* December 3, 2018

My day started as it usually did. I made a cup of coffee, steamed some milk, and toasted a slice of bread. Over this simple breakfast, I checked my email and read the *Wall Street Journal.* One headline caught my attention: "Why Perks No Longer Cut It for Workers," along with its byline: "The most successful companies give employees a sense of belonging." It was that final word that drew me in. As someone who introduces herself as an "Advocate for Inclusive Work-places," I read everything I can about diversity, inclusion, and belonging. In that article, I found the opening quote for this guidebook.

I became an advocate for inclusive workplaces for a simple reason: to support my leadership coaching clients, most of whom are women working in the male-dominated tech industry. By sharing cautionary tales about non-inclusive work situations, I hope to raise awareness of the challenges millions of employees face. I curate simple, everyday actions anyone can take to create more inclusive cultures, for my clients and so many other members of underrepresented groups.

What is an inclusive workplace? It's the kind of place where employees are thriving and doing their best work. Engagement survey scores are through the roof. People from different backgrounds, ethnicities, genders, sexual orien-tations, ages, and abilities are hired and set up for success—and they want their friends to work there too because their experience is so positive.

Inclusive workplaces foster a sense of belonging, which is critical to realizing the benefits of a diverse workforce. In a nutshell, these benefits are impressive. Study after study shows that diverse teams create more innovative solutions, they're more adept at solving difficult problems, and they achieve better financial success.[1]

Are you looking to build this kind of workplace? Are you trying to create a more diverse and inclusive workforce than you already have? If so, most experts will point to two high-level steps you can take to get that ball rolling.

Step one is to ensure your current employees feel included and supported to do their best work. Start by collecting their top concerns through company-wide surveys, then actively work to address any issues raised. Even better is to ask individuals this question and then take action: "What two changes would make it easier for you to do a great job?"[2]

In other words, make sure your house is in order before bringing in more talent from underrepresented groups. Otherwise, they won't stick around very long.

> Make sure your house is in order before bringing in more talent from underrepresented groups. Otherwise, they won't stick around very long.

Next, you'll want to cast a wider net during the hiring process. A critical mindset shift is to seek candidates beyond our typically homogeneous networks. By reaching out to people from underrepresented ethnicities and genders, with non-traditional educational backgrounds, with gaps on their resumes, or from older generations, we can attract more applicants for our job openings.

But there's more—much more—that we can do to bring job seekers from underrepresented groups into our hiring process. Plus there are steps to take to ensure our interviewing and onboarding processes are inclusive and equitable.

The rest of this guide provides actions you can take to help diversify your workforce.

One thing you won't find here is information about automated tools that remove or mitigate bias during the hiring process. While there are some products available, I decided not to write about them. Algorithms can't do it all, and I want this guide to raise awareness of the role we all can play in being more inclusive.

You also won't find legal advice. Employment law varies from country to country, from state to state. Any action you take upon the information in this guidebook is at your discretion. Please take steps to ensure that your hiring and recruiting process follows governing laws for your region.

As I wrote each chapter, I did my best to discuss the challenges facing all marginalized groups across many workplace settings. That said, my own experience as a white, straight, cisgender, able-bodied woman means that gender inequality is my entry point. Because I worked in the tech industry for over twenty-five years, most recently as a vice president of engineering at Adobe, tech is my greatest area of expertise. My personal experience is bound to influence my perspective, but I've done my best to highlight research and stories that reflect the experiences of other groups in other industries and model what it's like to be an ally to all marginalized groups.

During my writing process, I borrowed heavily from my book, *Better Allies: Everyday Actions to Create Inclusive, Engaging Workplaces.*

If you're interested in learning how to be a better ally for members of underrepresented groups beyond the hiring process, I encourage you to check it out. You'll learn to spot situations where you can create a more inclusive work culture, along with straightforward steps to take that will make a difference.

By creating a culture where all people can do their best work and thrive, you'll be better equipped to attract the best and brightest talent. The cream of the crop will want to work with and for you. Employees will share how good it is with their friends and whisper networks. The word will get out.

1

THE HIRING PIPELINE

The hiring pipeline is an easy scapegoat for why a workforce lacks diversity. You've probably heard the excuses. Maybe you've even made some of them yourself. I know I have.

"There aren't enough female candidates." "We don't get many people of color applying for jobs." "We'd hire them if we could find them." "We post a job and only men apply."

The list goes on.

Yet, people who are members of underrepresented groups are often bewildered. Many eager and qualified candidates, working hard to get hired, are passed over. They feel unnoticed. Invisible even.

It's more than anecdotal. The tech industry, in particular, has a quantifiable problem compared to other industries that employ software engineers. In 2015, LinkedIn measured gender equality across industries and discovered something interesting. Roughly one-third of software engineers employed in health care, government, education, and nonprofits were women, compared to just one-fifth in tech itself.[3]

Some might say there's "a higher bar" in tech than in other industries, and that tech companies don't want to "lower the bar" to hire members of underrepresented groups. This is just another excuse and a bigoted one at that. Joelle

Emerson, the founder of diversity and inclusion consultancy organization Paradigm, writes:

> *The concern about "lowering the bar" stems from an incorrect (and biased) belief that a company has a high bar designed to hire the best people, and the reason it hasn't hired more diverse people is that they aren't able to meet that bar. In fact, in many cases it's the opposite: companies have a poorly designed hiring bar that fails to adequately evaluate highly qualified, and often diverse, candidates.[4]*

I've experienced this poorly designed hiring bar firsthand. Early in my career, I interviewed for a software engineering job on the same day and at the same company as my partner, Tim. At that point, our resumes were almost identical. We'd graduated with computer science degrees from the same university. When we first entered the workforce, we'd worked at a research institute on the same project. We'd even published a technical paper together.

When Tim and I decided to move to Silicon Valley, we applied for jobs at many of the same companies, which was not surprising, given our common interests and experience.

What *was* surprising was what happened during one long day of interviews.

A large tech company brought us onsite to interview for software development roles. In side-by-side conference rooms, my partner and I talked with each person on the interview team. After someone interviewed Tim, they came to interview me, and vice versa. It went on for hours.

In our rental car on the way back to our hotel, we compared notes. That's when I discovered the unconscious bias that had been in play.

As Tim shared the tough questions he'd been asked, I was shocked. By contrast, my interviews were superficial and skirted any difficult technical topics. I couldn't believe the difference. In the few seconds it took the interviewers to close the door to the room Tim was in, take a few steps, and open the door to the room I was in, they lowered the bar. They did so before I'd said a word on my own behalf.

We both got job offers from that company, but there was no way I was joining a team that viewed me as a woman who lacked the same technical chops as a man. I declined, and I never looked back. I joined a different company and went on to build my career at places that valued my skills and talents regardless of my gender.

In addition to lowering the bar, companies find other ways to bungle the hiring process. Alison Wynn, a postdoctoral fellow at Stanford University's Clayman Institute for Gender Research, and Shelley Correll, a Stanford sociology professor, studied on-campus recruiting sessions for graduating STEM students. They found that many companies alienated women from the moment they walked in the door.[5] Instead of focusing on compelling work and advancement opportunities, the mostly male recruiters and engineers spoke about their companies' frat-like cultures, free food, dry cleaning, and other perks (many of which underscored the expectation that employees spend most of their life at the office). Their presentations included sexist jokes and imagery. Speakers often made comments that disparaged women or depicted them as sexualized objects instead of technical colleagues.

Makinde Adeagbo, a software engineer who has worked at Pinterest, Dropbox, and Facebook, shared this story of an appalling interview experience he had to endure:

*The technical founder/CEO walked into the room to ask a few technical questions. He was the author of a large, open source project. So, while I'd never met him before, I recognized his name and expected a challenging interview. Shockingly, his first question had nothing to do with technology. "Why do all the Black kids sit at the same table at school?" he asked. I was taken aback but tried to explain the social dynamics that might be at play. He followed with, "Why is it no longer okay to say n****r?" [I'd] never had that cutting word said to me and had a serious choice to make. Should I stand up and leave, or treat this as a teaching moment? It took mettle, but I chose the latter and gave the best 3 minute summary of 20th-century race relations that I could come up with. I finished the interview loop and went back to campus. When the recruiter called and congratulated me on getting an offer, I immediately declined, citing "severe cultural differences."* [6]

In case you're thinking that these are just isolated incidents, I've got a few more examples to share.

At a holiday party in December 2019, I caught up with a friend who recently took a sales job at a large tech company in San Francisco. Her new company has a stellar reputation for supporting women employees, and I couldn't wait to ask if the culture was everything she had hoped it would be. My friend said that, while it was great, it wasn't perfect. For example, one of her new colleagues confided that, during the interview process just a few months earlier, a vice president asked her if she had children. He then went on to ask if business travel would be a problem for her. Even if this question weren't illegal in the United States (and in many other countries), it's biased and inappropriate. [7]

In an interview with the *Washington Post*, college student Janeé Burch shared that even at historically black colleges like the one she attends, they are taught to tone down their natural hair when they go to job interviews.[8]

While the pipeline might be an easy excuse for why it's hard to hire people from underrepresented groups, I hope you're willing to think differently. Try to work to actively expand your pipeline *and* ensure you're being inclusive when interviewing these candidates.

The following chapters explore ideas for treating candidates equitably and strategies for hiring a more diverse workforce. Specifically, I cover:

- Chapter 2: Your Careers Page

- Chapter 3: Your Job Descriptions

- Chapter 4: Your Candidate Pool

- Chapter 5: Your Interview Process

- Chapter 6: Continue the Journey

Each chapter comes with a checklist of best practices to apply to your own hiring process. Ready to get started? Let's dive in.

2

YOUR CAREERS PAGE

A careers page is one of the first places a potential employee will visit to learn more about a company's culture, open positions, benefits, and advancement opportunities. If your company is serious about attracting a diverse pool of candidates, make certain this page is welcoming to them.

Obvious? Sure. But doing so can be easier said than done. Sometimes people aren't aware of how their careers page might be perceived. They may think it's another employee's responsibility to ensure the page is effective. Or they might face pushback when requesting edits to make it more inclusive because of higher priority website change requests.

I've seen all of this when working on consulting projects for companies who want to attract and hire underrepresented candidates. To help my clients identify changes to their careers page, I often follow this guidance from the National Center for Women in Information Technology (NCWIT), which I modified slightly to include other underrepresented groups and non-tech fields:[9]

- Do you use language and images to convey that people from marginalized groups belong at your workplace?

- Do you emphasize an inclusive work culture?

- Do you showcase how your company's work is contributing to social good? The social value of work can attract candidates from marginalized groups.

While most of my clients tend to do well in these three areas, there is always something for them to improve. Some of those areas for improvement are more surprising than others, as I'm about to share with you.

Use diverse, welcoming images

First, look at the photos on your company's careers page. Do the photos show employees of all kinds thriving within the company? Or are they full of young white dudes having a good time?

Here are some issues that I've flagged for my clients, all from their career web pages. (I wish I could show them to you, but I don't think these companies would give me permission to reprint them. Instead, these descriptions will have to suffice.)

- A photo of a dozen people carrying paintball rifles. Ten men and one woman were standing and smiling. Another woman was sitting on the ground, not looking happy at all.

- A photo of employees enjoying a dance party, in what looked like a mosh pit. One man was on his back, held up by the others who jostled him around the pit. The red flag? As a woman, the last thing I'd want to do at a company event is to have others' hands all over my body, potentially even groping me. If this was how the company had fun, count me out.

- One company had a nice rotation of photos showing employees in different settings, yet the website always displayed the same one first: two white male cyclists wearing jerseys with the company logo. Why not lead with a photo showing more diversity?

Before you decide your own page is perfectly fine, put yourself in the shoes of an applicant from an under-represented group. Imagine how a woman, a person of color, an older worker, a person with a disability, or a single parent would feel seeing the images on your careers page. Would they see people who look nothing like them, engaging in activities that broadcast an uninviting culture? Or would they see people from a variety of backgrounds in settings that showcase their enjoyment at work and value to the company? Candidates need to be able to envision themselves working somewhere, and seeing their own experience reflected through photos is a crucial way to do that.

That said, be genuine and authentic. Use photos of your employees in a way that represents your demographics. In other words, don't try to deceive candidates by showcasing more diversity than you actually have. If you have only one (or a small number of people) of a given demographic, don't feature them as though they were the norm.

To be fully transparent, consider putting your diversity statistics on your careers page, along with an explanation of what you're doing to improve them. Do this not just for the overall employee population, but realize that many candidates will also look for diversity on your company's leadership page. If your executive team is mostly male and pale, explain any goals you have for improving representation there, too.

Wondering what to do if you don't have a diverse workforce at all?

First up, don't use stock photography. It may be a tempting solution, but candidates can easily do an image search online and find that your "employee" is a model who appears on many job sites. (Yes, this happens. In doing research for this guide, I quickly spotted a stock photo of a Black male model featured as though he were an employee on a Fortune 500 company's careers page.[10])

Secondly, you're going to have to emphasize how welcoming and inclusive you are through text, not photos. I'll explore this in the next section.

One last thing about photos. Keep in mind that candidates may use assistive technology such as screen readers. To help them understand what your images depict, be sure to add descriptions with HTML alt tags or in captions underneath the photos.

Describe an inclusive culture

While photos are important, don't forget about the power of language in making people feel like they belong ... or not.

In describing their organizational culture, one of my clients, a small start-up, emphasized the importance of their after-hour LAN parties. I have to admit I didn't know what a LAN party was, so I searched online and discovered that it's when a local area network (LAN) is used to connect people playing multiplayer video games. At the time, the Entertainment Software Association reported that about half of all computer/video gamers were women, but this ratio dropped to around 15 percent with massive multiplayer games.[11] This company might have been unintentionally eliminating female candidates by nurturing this aspect of their culture and emphasizing it on their careers page.

While you shouldn't hide important aspects of your company's culture, be sure to highlight things that show a commitment to creating an inclusive workplace. Zapier, a web app automation company, does so with the following statement:

We're dedicated to building a warm, open, and inclusive work environment—one that's safe for people of all backgrounds. To this end, when you join our team, you agree to a code of conduct. And our steps to improve diversity and inclusion at Zapier are published in a public changelog.[12]

Another way to show a commitment to an inclusive culture is by offering resource or affinity groups for underrepresented employees. If these exist at your organization, be loud and proud about them on your careers page. For example, here's how the Massachusetts Institute of Technology (MIT) describes their groups:

Employee Resource Groups (ERGs) are employee-led groups formed around common interests, issues and/or a common bond or background.

ERG members create a positive work environment at MIT by actively contributing to the Institute's mission, values and efforts specific to inclusion, such as recruitment and retention. All of MIT's ERGs are open to any employee.

MIT is pleased to support the following Employee Resource Groups.
- *African, Black, American, Caribbean (ABAC) ERG*
- *Asian Pacific American (APA) ERG*
- *Disabilities ERG*
- *Latino ERG*

- *Lesbian, Bisexual, Gay, Transgender Queer (LBGTQ) ERG*
- *Millennials ERG*
- *Women in Technology (WIT) ERG*[13]

Welcome all candidates

Think about how you describe the kind of candidates you're looking for. Are you being welcoming to people from diverse backgrounds, ethnicities, sexual orientations, ages, and abilities? I especially appreciate the inclusive way Change.org does this:

> *Your coworkers are high-impact, low-ego, and have a deep respect for our members. We expect you to be the same.*
>
> *All qualified applicants will receive consideration for employment without regard to race, colour, national origin, religion, sexual orientation, gender, gender identity, age, physical disability, or length of time spent unemployed.*[14]

Did you notice that last phrase? "Length of time spent unemployed." This company encourages job seekers to apply even with resume gaps. Here's why I like that a lot.

Between 2008 and 2013, one in four Americans in their fifties lost their jobs. Many gave up looking after that economic downturn because they assumed a lapse in employment would be held against them.

To attract workers who may have been forced out of work during that time, as well as others who have taken a break in their career for health or caregiving reasons, make it clear that you won't hold it against them.

Veterans are another group that you may want to specifically welcome to apply to your openings. Waste management company Republic Services prominently displays a button labeled "Veterans" on their careers page. Clicking it leads to a page showcasing veterans who are their employees, along with this message:

Hiring our Heroes

> *Republic Services has built its success on 5 values including Respect, Responsibility, Reliability, Resourcefulness and a Relentless focus on taking care of our customers. We have found that these values align well with those who are transitioning from military service. We actively recruit and hire recently transitioned military as well as those long discharged from active duty. Republic Services has a proven track record of hiring and developing those who have served as we value the skills, experience and operational excellence you bring to our organization and your commitment to a better tomorrow.*

> *Republic Services provides training to help ensure a successful transition from military service to a career at Republic Services, and our culture of success through engaged, diverse teams helps all military veterans succeed in a variety of positions, including operations managers, maintenance technicians, drivers, and sales representatives.*[15]

Here's one more idea for being inclusive on your careers page. (I've saved the best for last.) **Encourage candidates to apply even if they don't meet all the requirements.**

You've probably heard about a now-famous internal Hewlett-Packard study that found that women applied for a promotion only when they believed they met 100 percent of the qualifications listed for the job, while men applied when they thought they could meet 60 percent of the job requirements.[16]

Hewlett-Packard's findings have been validated by other research. In *How to Lead*, Jo Owen describes how men applied for head teaching roles when they thought they were 50 percent ready, while women wanted to be nearer to 100 percent ready before taking on the responsibility.[17] Leadership development trainer Tara Mohr dug deeper and found that the problem isn't a lack of confidence in women applicants. She polled more than a thousand men and women and found that both genders were likely to avoid applying for jobs if they believed they didn't meet the qualifications. In an article for *Harvard Business Review*, Tara writes:

> *They didn't see the hiring process as one where advocacy, relationships, or a creative approach to framing one's expertise could overcome not having the skills and experiences outlined in the job qualifications. What held them back from applying was not a mistaken perception about themselves, but a mistaken perception about the hiring process.*[18]

Want to attract more candidates for your open roles, especially for those that are hard to fill? Consider adding this one sentence to your job ads, like website tool company Webflow:

> *We'd love to hear from you—even if you don't meet 100% of the requirements.*[19]

Be transparent about your interview process

As software company Automattic found when they surveyed job applicants: "It's important for women job searchers to know what the hiring process looks like when they are applying because of non-work-related commitments many have."[20] I bet their finding applies to other genders, too.

As a result of this research, Autommatic created a page that clearly outlines its hiring process for software developers. It includes a four-to-six hour coding challenge and a paid, flexible, part-time trial period.[21]

Procter & Gamble is also transparent about their process, outlining what happens during the application, assessment, interview, and offer steps. They also take the opportunity to acknowledge some candidates may need accommodations due to disabilities:

> *To ensure that everybody who is interested in joining our team has equal opportunity and ability to start that journey, we have made sure our hiring process is flexible and accessible. From the application to interviews, our team will adapt to your needs and what works best to help you show us your best. To learn more about the P&G Disability Accommodation process, click here.*[22]

Want to attract candidates who care about diversity and belonging? Consider clearly stating that your interview process includes asking how a candidate has supported creating a more diverse and inclusive team or community in the past. Doing so can help demonstrate that your company cares about equity and inclusion and that you expect all new hires to help move that needle forward.

(More on this in Chapter 5, including questions to ask to screen for inclusive attitudes and experiences during interviews.)

Share your values

Many organizations have value statements representing what they stand for, what they value, what they care about. To be transparent with candidates, list your value statements on the careers page.

My former employer, Adobe, describes four core values on its website, including my personal favorite: "Involved—Inclusive, open and actively engaged with our customers, partners, employees and the communities we serve."[23]

Of course, if you have any concerns that your values might turn off job seekers from underrepresented groups, you may need to rethink those values. One example that comes to mind is Uber's "Always be hustlin'" value from Travis Kalanick's tenure. To reflect the culture and approach they would need to responsibly grow their business moving forward, their second CEO, Dara Khosrowshahi, replaced all of the previous values with new ones:[24]

Original	Revised
Customer obsession (Start with what is best for the customer.) **Make magic** (Seek breakthroughs that will stand the test of time.) **Big bold bets** (Take risks and plant seeds that are five to ten years out.) **Inside out** (Find the gap between popular perception and reality.) **Champion's mind-set** (Put everything you have on the field to overcome adversity and get Uber over the finish line.) **Optimistic leadership** (Be inspiring.)	**We build globally, we live locally.** We harness the power and scale of our global operations to deeply connect with the cities, communities, drivers and riders that we serve, every day. **We are customer obsessed.** We work tirelessly to earn our customers' trust and business by solving their problems, maximizing their earnings or lowering their costs. We surprise and delight them. We make short-term sacrifices for a lifetime of loyalty.

(continued on the next page)

Original (continued)	Revised (continued)
Superpumped (The world is a puzzle to be solved with enthusiasm.)	**We celebrate differences.** We stand apart from the average. We ensure people of diverse backgrounds feel welcome. We encourage different opinions and approaches to be heard, then we come together and build.
Be an owner, not a renter (Revolutions are won by true believers.)	
Meritocracy and toe-stepping (The best idea always wins. Don't sacrifice truth for social cohesion and don't hesitate to challenge the boss.)	**We do the right thing.** Period. **We act like owners.** We seek out problems and we solve them. We help each other and those who matter to us. We
Let builders build (People must be empowered to build things.)	have a bias for action and accountability. We finish what
Always be hustlin' (Get more done with less, working longer, harder, and smarter, not just two out of three.)	we start and we build Uber to last. And when we make mistakes, we'll own up to them.
Celebrate cities (Everything we do is to make cities better.)	**We persevere.** We believe in the power of grit. We don't seek the easy path. We look for the
Be yourself (Each of us should be authentic.)	toughest challenges and we push. Our collective resilience is our secret weapon.
Principled confrontation (Sometimes the world and institutions need to change in order for the future to be ushered in.)	**We value ideas over hierarchy.** We believe that the best ideas can come from anywhere, both inside and outside our company. Our job is to seek out those ideas, to shape and improve them through candid debate, and to take them from concept to action.
	We make big bold bets. Sometimes we fail, but failure makes us smarter. We get back up, we make the next bet, and we go!

If your values need to be revised or updated to meet your needs going forward and to help attract more candidates from underrepresented groups, consider keeping the list short and to the point. (Let's face it. Uber's new list of values is quite long.) A concise list will help employees remember the values, share them during the interview process, and act on them as they go about their day-to-day work. For example, I appreciate how succinct Salesforce's core values are: Trust, Customer Success, Innovation, and Equality.[25]

Concise Core Values

The best core values are brief but comprehensive, making it easy for employees to remember them, refer to them during the interview process, and act on them daily.

If your company contributes to social good, say so

As NCWIT points out, the social value of work can attract candidates from marginalized groups. If your company is mission-led, with a goal of being economically successful while also having a positive impact on society, be sure this is emphasized on the careers page. Here's how Visa describes its mission on a "Life at Visa" section of its careers site:

Be part of an incredible team driving economic growth in even the most remote parts of the world, with a goal of bringing financial literacy and digital commerce to over 500 million unbanked consumers by 2020. Take advantage of Volunteer Time Off (VTO) and our matching gifts program and give back to our communities.[26]

Alternatively, if your company doesn't have such a mission, look for ways to appeal to candidates who want to contribute to social good. Does your organization offer volunteering opportunities? Do you have a mobile blood donation center on-site on a regular basis? Do you have customers who utilize your product offerings for their own mission-driven strategic goals? If so, say so.

Here's another idea. I remember speaking with a company that launches satellites to collect data from space. As I asked about their customers, I heard inspiring stories. One utilized weather data to improve farming yields. Another relied on maritime traffic data to go after pirates. I encouraged them to showcase these stories on their careers page to share how they help customers make a positive impact in the world.

Emphasize employee benefits

Last but not least, review the language used to describe employee benefits on your company's careers page. While I recommend you have a link to a complete description of your benefits, highlight those that are particularly important to members of underrepresented groups. Here are some examples:

Benefits to Highlight

- Parental leave. And not just for the person who gave birth. (Automattic found that women review a careers page looking almost exclusively for red flags. One is offering only maternity leave, not paternity leave.[27])

- Adoption assistance.

- On-site childcare.

- Eldercare.

- Domestic partner benefits.

- Trans-inclusive healthcare.

- Reproductive health coverage.

- Mentorship and sponsorship programs.

While applicable to all, these benefits are especially important to women, who are the primary caregivers in our society.[28]

Whether through photos, the language used to describe your company's culture and social impact, employee benefits, or other means, members of marginalized groups will evaluate your company by your careers page. Think about the messages you want to send, and ensure that your website reinforces them.

Checklist for Your Careers Page

☐ Explore the photos on your company's careers page.
   What message do they send to candidates? Do they
   show real employees, representing the true diversity
   within your company? Do they have captions or HTML
   alt tags for people using screen readers?

☐ Review how you describe the culture of your company.
   Do you list employee resource groups and other
   offerings that demonstrate a commitment to an
   inclusive workplace?

☐ Look at how you describe the kinds of candidates
   you're looking for. Are there changes to make to be
   more inclusive of people of different genders,
   ethnicities, religions, sexual orientations, ages, and
   abilities? Can you be actively inclusive of candidates
   who have spent time unemployed? Do you welcome
   veterans? Do you encourage people to apply even if
   they don't meet 100 percent of the requirements?

☐ Are you transparent about your interview process?

☐ Think about how your company or customers
   contribute to social good. Is this explained clearly on
   your careers page?

☐ Do you emphasize employee benefits, especially those
   important to caregivers?

3

YOUR JOB DESCRIPTIONS

Let's move on to job descriptions themselves and the role they play in attracting a diverse candidate pool for your open positions. As in the previous chapter, I recommend starting with guidance from NCWIT:

- Are all of the criteria listed necessary for doing this job well?

- Do any of the criteria reflect typical assumptions about the "kind of person" you think usually does this job?

- Do you provide a way to account for important life experiences that may not show up on traditional resumes but that can indicate a likelihood for success in this job?

- Does the language in the description or advertisement subtly reflect gender or racial stereotypes/preferences (e.g., language such as "high-powered," "results-driven," "action-oriented," "people person")?

- Do you include and value criteria such as "ability to work on a diverse team or with a diverse range of people"?[29]

This list is a great starting point for writing job descriptions. Let's dive into some concrete examples that put them into action.

Avoid biased language

This may seem obvious and straightforward, yet biased language can easily creep into job postings. Words such as "guy," "craftsman," "he/him/his," and "right-hand man" may seem innocuous, but are actually exclusionary. Using other masculine-coded words like "aggressive," "competitive," and "individual" can deter women from applying.[30]

I also recommend avoiding sports terminology because not everyone grew up playing or watching these sports. Reading a job description with baseball, basketball, or US football phrases, for example, can be a turn-off or just confusing to someone not familiar with them. Here are some examples:

- "Seeking a quarterback to join our sales group."

- "This role is for someone who can step up to the plate and hit it out of the park."

- "The ideal candidate has a track record of entrepreneurial home runs."

There are also blatant examples of jobs being described for a certain gender or race. For example, "Vice President HR (male only),"[31] "Account Manager Sales (female candidates only),"[32] and "Business Development Manager (preferably Caucasian)."[33]

News flash: Avoiding biased or downright discriminatory language can help you be welcoming to a wider candidate pool. Use an automated online tool to find instances, or get help from a keen-eyed editor.

To show you what this might look like, here's a job description from the "Tech Companies That Only Hire Men" blog, edited to be less biased:[34]

Before	After
Entrepreneurial Minded Small Business seeks "Fireman" Operations Associate	Entrepreneurial Minded Small Business seeks Operations Associate
Aggressive, assertive, "get stuff done"/"take charge" type personality sought for a position of operations manager and assistant to Chief Operating Officer of dot com technology company.	Organized, motivated person sought for a position of operations manager and assistant to Chief Operating Officer of dot com technology company.

Limit the number of requirements to five

I'm going to embarrass myself now. As I think back on job descriptions I wrote during my twenty-five years working in tech, I started each one by copying a similar job post and then adding new skills and experience needed for the role. Maybe I deleted a requirement or two, but overall, my job descriptions became unnecessarily long.

I also bet that all of them listed "bachelor's degree or higher" as a requirement. It was a convention to attract a certain caliber of talent. Yet, in reality, the skills needed to perform many of these jobs could have just as easily been gained via life experience or some nontraditional education.

Here's why bloated job descriptions are a problem. In the previous chapter, I shared research showing that candidates, especially women, are likely to avoid applying for a job if they don't believe they meet all the requirements listed. This means that superfluous bullet points may cause great candidates to weed themselves out.

Given this research, review job descriptions you're planning to post and remove any requirements that aren't truly necessary for the roles they describe. In fact, I recommend aiming for five at most. While it's not a magic number, it does set an aspirational goal for minimizing job requirements.

Apply this same rule to the number of years of experience required in particular skills. Ask yourself: If a strong candidate came along with only two years working with Java, would you hire them even if your job posting says you require three to five years? If your answer is yes, you shouldn't list a required number of years at all.

Likewise, cut the "nice to have" and "preferred" requirements unless you truly need this experience (in which case, call them out as "full" requirements).

To continue editing the job description down to its bare minimum, remove any skills that a new hire can easily learn on the job.

Last but not least, think about whether you need candidates to possess a certain university diploma, advanced degree, or professional certification. In recent years, many companies, including IBM, Google, and Apple, have stopped requiring college degrees.[35] I recommend not listing them in your job descriptions either unless they're absolutely required to be successful in the role.

If you feel like paring down job postings is "lowering the bar," check yourself. What we're doing here is editing writing that's often swollen and needlessly intimidating. Removing "preferred" items doesn't open a company up to a flood of unqualified candidates; rather, it forces the company to present a clearer picture of what it truly needs from the person who'll fill this role.

To summarize, here's a simple checklist of what I've covered so far in this chapter:

How to improve a job description

- ☐ Drop "preferred" requirements, degrees, and certifications (unless truly needed).

- ☐ Remove biased language.

- ☐ Combine similar or duplicate requirements.

- ☐ Remove skills that can easily be taught on the job.

- ☐ For everything else: ask, "If an otherwise perfect candidate came along without this experience, would we still hire them?" If so, cut it. Aim for a maximum of five requirements.

With a simpler set of requirements, you should attract candidates who might otherwise not apply if they don't meet every single requirement on the list.

On the next page, you'll find an example of how I took a client's bloated posting (for a software automation engineer) and applied this checklist to simplify it to only four requirements.

Before	After
4-6 years experience in hands-on Quality Assurance testing and release of multi-tier applications with multiple browsers (IE, Firefox, Mozilla, Safari, Netscape) and platforms (Windows, Linux)	Experience in hands-on Quality Assurance testing and release of multi-tier applications with multiple browsers and multiple platforms
Expert level load testing and stress testing skills in a web 2.0 environment	Experience leading web application test projects from planning to release
Deep knowledge of automation tools and frameworks	Load testing and stress testing skills in a web 2.0 environment
Proficient in programming and scripting using Python, Selenium	Experience with Python, Selenium, SQL, automation tools and automation frameworks
Experience leading web application test projects from planning to release	
Expert understanding of QA methodology and the software development lifecycle	
Ability to develop a clear and concise testing strategy and craft robust, comprehensive test plans to verify functionality	
Experience with automated tests	
Ability to work in an exciting environment and meet bold deadlines	
Excellent organization and interpersonal skills	
Working knowledge of SQL	
Strong verbal and written communication skills	
Motivated and assertive in learning and owning projects	
BS or equivalent experience in Computer Science or related Engineering field preferred	

For managerial positions, seek experience with diverse teams

If you're hiring a manager or a team lead, do you want to attract candidates who care about diversity, some of whom may be from underrepresented groups themselves? Consider including "experience hiring and leading diverse teams" as a requirement. Send a clear message that this experience is both relevant and desired.

Before	After
Ability to influence people across the organization	Ability to influence people across the organization
Ability to coach your reports to grow a high-performance team	Ability to coach your reports to grow a high-performance team
	Experience hiring and leading diverse teams

For technical roles, don't require open source experience (unless it's truly required)

In certain tech circles, contributing to open source projects is a badge of honor because it involves writing code that others can use for free and build upon. People who spend free time coding are sometimes seen as more "serious" engineers. When hiring software engineers, it can be tempting to look for people with open source experience because of the credibility that comes along with it. Yet 95 percent of open source contributors are men.[36] The landscape can be harsh— with a lack of role models for women and nonbinary individuals, competing personal and family priorities, a combative hacker ethic, "flame wars," and the difficulty women face when receiving adequate recognition for contributions. Understandably, many women choose not to participate.

If open source experience is a strict requirement for a position, then, of course, it should be listed as a requirement in the job description. Otherwise, don't mention it.

Before	After
3-5 years open source experience preferred	

For technical roles, consider whether you really need to evaluate candidates' GitHub profiles

Some job sites ask technical candidates for their GitHub profiles. Recruiters and hiring managers can then explore the candidates' source code firsthand to evaluate the code they've published, the projects they've forked, and the commits they've landed. Sounds good on the surface, but here's the rub: It assumes candidates are writing code in their free time (and aren't busy working a second job to pay the bills, handling childcare responsibilities, or balancing other demands on their time). It's basically another sign of privilege, not technical prowess.

So, before you ask to see someone's GitHub activity, ask yourself if you truly need to.

Checklist for Your Job Descriptions

☐ Can you find any biased language? E.g., Words that imply the candidate is a certain gender or from a particular background. "Man" words ("right-hand man," "superman," etc). Or other masculine-coded words like "aggressive," "competitive," and "assertive." Or sports terminology. How would you edit it to be less biased?

☐ Drop "preferred" requirements, degrees, and certifications (unless truly needed).

☐ Combine similar or duplicate requirements to simplify the description.

☐ Remove skills that can easily be taught on the job.

☐ For managerial positions, do you require prior experience leading diverse teams? If not, consider adding it to attract candidates who value diversity.

☐ For technical roles, do you require open source experience? Or a candidate's GitHub profile? Unless it's truly required, remove it.

☐ For everything else: ask, "If an otherwise perfect candidate came along without this experience, would we still hire them?" If so, cut it. Aim for a maximum of five requirements.

4

YOUR CANDIDATE POOL

At the Stanford VMware Women's Leadership Lab, researchers frequently hear comments like, "I'd love to hire more women, but when I post a job, they don't apply. They're not interested" and "there just aren't enough qualified women to do the job." Each time, they're reminded of the art of fishing: If you don't catch a fish, you don't blame the fish. You change your technique.[37]

In this chapter, I'll share some techniques you can use to diversify candidate pools. Experienced applicants from marginalized groups are out there, and attracting them to your company is not the impossible task that pipeline-blamers think it is.

Diversify your network

Did you know most people have largely homogenous professional networks? For example, a report from the Kapor Center for Social Impact states that 75 percent of white people don't have any people of color in their social network.[38] Furthermore, according to the 2017 "Women in the Workplace" study by LeanIn.Org and McKinsey & Company: "Women are more than five times more likely to rely on a network that is mostly female."[39]

Homogeneous networks form because of the way we network. Herminia Ibarra, a professor of organizational behavior at the London Business School, says, "Left to our own devices … we produce networks that are 'just like me,' convenience networks."[40]

This makes sense because common interests tend to fuel networks. Let's face it, we meet new people because of our shared hobbies or other interests. While I was working as vice president of engineering at Adobe, I joined the knitting club in our San Francisco office. Meeting over lunch on Wednesdays, we got to know each other while knitting baby blankets and hats for a local nonprofit. I loved it. But, guess how many male colleagues I met via the knitting group? Zero. Sure, there are men who enjoy knitting, but none joined our group.

Building a professional network across lines of difference can prove difficult, especially when it involves getting outside our comfort zone. While not impossible, it can be challenging. Outside of work, men tend to hang out with their male coworkers, perhaps grabbing a beer after work, playing poker or a round of golf, or going to a ball game together. By contrast, women are more likely to spend time with non-work friends outside of the office, such as book club members, fellow volunteers for a nonprofit, members of a religious organization, or, if we have kids, other parents from playgroups and school.[41] For women who handle the lion's share of housework and childcare, networking can be extra challenging. Home responsibilities can make it tough to pull off attending evening events or out-of-town conferences.

The upshot: Men network with men, women with women. Engineers network with other engineers, and marketers with other marketers. We want people who understand us, and instinctively know that people who are similar to us are likely to relate to our challenges and triumphs. It's human nature.

Unfortunately, "just like me" networks can have a negative impact on creating diverse, inclusive workplaces. Those who are involved in hiring new staff naturally look to the people who are part of their professional networks, because they know and trust them, but when those networks are homogenous, this translates to favoring and advocating for folks like themselves. Depending on referrals is standard, and if those referrals come from a homogeneous network, it results in just hiring more homogeneity.

There's an adage I love: Build your network before you need it. As software engineer Samantha Geitz shared on Twitter:

> *You have to build a network for diversity. This takes YEARS... I'll tell you how you can start today. Follow 10 people on Twitter who aren't white dudes. Chat with them every so often. Do it without an agenda.*[42]

All of this begs the question: How will you start building a more diverse network today, before your next hiring push? (For ideas on how to do so, check out my book, *Better Allies: Everyday Actions to Create Inclusive, Engaging Workplaces*.)

Vary where you post your openings

As a female CEO, Kendall Tucker thought it would be easy to find strong female candidates for openings at her company, Polis. But she was receiving 95 percent male applicants for all job postings.

To diversify her team, she employed a number of strategies. While much of what she did was familiar territory for me, she did point out one approach I hadn't thought of before: "Post on a variety of job sites to get a diverse candidate pool."

It turns out that for positions at Polis, job postings on LinkedIn attracted up to 90 percent male engineering applicants, where Angellist, Indeed, Glassdoor, and Google attracted more balanced candidate pools.[43]

Depending on your hiring goals, you may want to leverage job sites with specific niches, such as people returning to work after a gap, older workers, and women who want to work remotely.

Don't forget about advertising or posting on sites where people in these demographics may spend time. Think about conferences, meetups, alumni networks, and other professional resources.

Surprisingly, Automattic found that many women and non-binary job candidates use Stack Overflow to look for jobs, even though Stack Overflow reported in 2019 that only 11 percent of their users were women.[44] As Automattic shared, "We had previously advertised on that platform and dis-continued it based on the demographics of applications it drove; diversity of applicants was even lower than the already too-low industry average." However based on their findings, they reversed their decision and began posting job openings there again.[45]

Depending on your company, location, and the position you're posting, you may attract a diversity of applicants through a single site. But why not cast a wider net?

Tap your current workforce

Ask employees to recommend former colleagues from under-represented groups. Encourage everyone, and I mean everyone—not just people who are from underrepresented groups themselves—to dig deep into their networks.

Pinterest employed this tactic and saw amazing results. Instead of just asking for "referrals"—which tend to be drawn from people's naturally homogeneous networks—the company requested engineering referrals for women and candidates from underrepresented ethnic backgrounds specifically. They gathered these referrals during a six-week "challenge" period, a device for adding excitement and making the entire employee base feel invested in increasing diversity. During those six weeks, Pinterest saw a 24 percent increase in the number of women referred and 55 times as many people from underrepresented ethnic backgrounds.[46]

Another technique for encouraging your employees to dig deep into their networks and focus on underrepresented demographics is to hold a sourcing jam or party. Here's how it works:

- Invite them to a meeting, provide food and beverages, and play some upbeat music.

- Discuss your goals for improving diversity and the demographics you want to focus on.

- Review open positions and suggest searches each person can do on their LinkedIn network or other social sites. The important thing is to have employees run these searches on their networks to get a richer set of candidates than if a recruiter were to do so.

- Share template messages for each person to send to get candidates from their networks interested, even intrigued, in your roles. This last step should not be skipped. Response rates should go up dramatically compared to a recruiter cold-emailing those same candidates.[47]

Looking for yet another idea? Offer a referral bonus for candidates from underrepresented demographics, or a larger amount if you have a referral bonus program already in place. It can incentivize people who otherwise might feel too busy to reach out to their networks and make recommendations.

To encourage employees to continue to refer people from diverse backgrounds even after the sourcing push, check back in and thank them. Let them know how their referrals made out. Even if one or more of their referrals weren't hired, let them know their effort was appreciated.

Encourage employees to be visible

Here's a secret weapon I learned from one of my consulting clients, who asked me to identify ways to increase the number of women on their software engineering team. My first step was to review their current demographics, and I found that they were in better shape than most tech companies. When I asked the vice president of engineering how they had hired so many women, he smiled and said he knew exactly why. There was a manager on his staff who frequently spoke at tech conferences and local women-in-tech meetups. After each of her presentations, they would get an influx of resumes from women engineers. These job seekers must have been inspired by her talk. They saw someone like themselves being successful at the company and decided to apply.

Think about your employees from underrepresented groups, and take stock of who is already visible externally. Think of public speakers, podcasters, bloggers, or social media influencers. Are there actions you can take to support them being even more visible? Can they include a brief

"We're hiring" message or encourage job seekers to reach out to them?

Next, think about employees from underrepresented demographics who would be good ambassadors for your organization. Ask them if they want to do more speaking or writing externally, and set them up for success with coaching, classes or other professional development opportunities.

If you decide to utilize this secret weapon, I have one word of caution. Any time you ask an employee to take on additional work that will benefit your organization, be sure to recognize and reward them for it. Being visible takes time, and it should be prioritized along with the rest of their responsibilities, not just heaped on top of an already full plate.

Insist on a diverse pool

In 2002, the National Football League instituted the Rooney Rule, which states that all teams are required to interview at least one candidate of color for all head coaching and senior football operation openings.[48] In 2016 film director J. J. Abrams created a hiring policy for his production company, Bad Robot, that required that women and people of color be considered for writing, directing, and acting jobs in a way that's proportional to their representation in the U.S. population.[49] Amazon and Microsoft have adopted similar tactics when hiring for open positions.[50] When PayPal started requiring at least one candidate from an underrepresented racial demographic be considered for every open position at the director level and above, they increased diversity at the vice president level by more than 5 percent.[51]

One of the best ways to ensure that candidates from underrepresented groups actually get hired at your company is to craft a policy that makes finding and interviewing them mandatory. It turns out that the most effective policy is to extend the Rooney Rule to require at least two candidates from the underrepresented group you are focused on.[52]

As you craft the right hiring policy for your needs, I hope you apply it at all levels of your organization—and not just at the entry-level where it might be easier to find candidates from underrepresented groups.

In Chapter 5, I'll explain how diverse interview teams complement the Rooney Rule, helping companies not only interview candidates from a diverse pool but also hire them.

Understand the journey

I regularly mentor women undergraduates who are considering careers in tech. One of my mentees, Maria, was a college senior from East Los Angeles, a densely populated, working-class neighborhood. She was the first in her family to go to college, and when I met her, she was studying computer science at an Ivy League school. She's smart, driven, and imaginative, and I'm excited to see where her career will take her.

Want to know how Maria spent her summers during college? No tech internships for her. Instead, she worked at a children's day camp near her home in L.A.

She didn't pursue internships during the time she spent on campus either. When I asked Maria why, she said, "I didn't think I was qualified. Plus, I was too busy working my job at the school cafeteria to fit in interviews." That on-campus job was Maria's priority because she needed the income to make ends meet.

Does not having a tech internship make her less gifted as a programmer, or less able to grasp how to submit a pull request for a large code base? Of course not. But it *may* make her ever-so-slightly less appealing to recruiters at first glance.

Similarly, as I learned from Minda Harts in her book, *The Memo,* counselors across the U.S. steer high school students of color to junior colleges instead of four-year institutions. For those students who are also the first generation in their family to attend college, they lack guidance in navigating the options. They tend to default to following their counselor's advice.[53]

Here's why this can be a problem. When hiring recent college grads, many people make huge assumptions about students who haven't attended name-brand schools or pursued certain experiences, without ever asking why. Until you face a situation in which one of them says, "Well, I wanted to do that, but here's why I couldn't," you might be unaware of this ingrained bias.

Instead of excluding someone because they didn't hit some mark, work to understand their journey.

Checklist for Your Candidate Pool

☐ Identify where you advertise your job openings. If it tends to be only one or two job sites, think about how you could cast a wider net.

☐ Are you tapping your current workforce to recommend candidates from underrepresented groups? Do you offer an incentive for referring them? Do you hold sourcing parties to get more referrals? Do you keep your employees informed about the status of their referrals?

☐ Most of us have homogeneous networks, which lead to hiring homogeneity. Think about your network and steps you can take to diversify it before you need to hire from it.

☐ Do you encourage current employees from underrepresented groups to be visible externally? Can you do more to support them?

☐ Do you have a mandate or quota for interviewing people from underrepresented groups?

☐ Are you open to candidates who haven't had the expected journey of highly-selective universities, internships, name-brand company experience, etc?

5

YOUR INTERVIEW PROCESS

Bias can too easily creep into the interview process like it did on that day my partner and I interviewed at the same company. There's research showing the impact of that bias. Resumes with African American–sounding names receive 50 percent fewer callbacks than resumes with white-sounding names. Candidates with accents, women, and working mothers are all rated less favorably than their peers.[54] Naturally, these biases lead to fewer hires of members of marginalized groups.

Then there's culture fit, and the age-old interview debrief question of, "Would you want to grab a beer with them?" Or, "Would you want to hang out with them during a long airport layover?"

Back in the 1980s, culture fit and "chemistry" were all the rage. They sprang from the idea that if companies hired employees whose personalities and values aligned with organizational strategy, those employees would feel more invested in their jobs and become more loyal. Skills were important, but cultivating a workforce of like-minded people ran a close second. Over time, however, "culture fit" became code for something else: passing the friendship test. The whole "grab a beer" scenario prompted decision-makers to begin thinking of "culture fit" as relating to likeability, personal similarities, and chemistry with the interviewer. It gave them license to hire people they wanted to spend time with and pass over people who might've been ideal for the job but clashed with their leadership styles.[55]

Patty McCord, a human resources consultant and former chief talent officer at Netflix, points out the following about hiring for culture fit: "You end up with this big, homogenous culture where everybody looks alike, everybody thinks alike, and everybody likes drinking beer at 3 o'clock in the afternoon with the bros."[56]

Fortunately, things are changing.

I remember attending a panel where Jeffrey Siminoff, who was then head of diversity at Twitter, made a truly memorable comment. "If I hear that a candidate isn't a culture fit, I ask if they could be a culture add." Right on.

Hear someone say that a candidate isn't a culture fit? Ask if they'd be a culture add.

In a similar vein, Aubrey Blanche, global head of diversity and belonging at Atlassian, recommends asking, "What will this candidate bring that we don't currently have on the team?"[57] Atlassian also has shifted its focus from "culture fit" to "values fit." It helps recruiters hire people who share the company's goals, but not necessarily the viewpoints or backgrounds of the interview team.[58]

Prove it again bias

Another kind of bias that can show up in the interview process is "prove it again" bias. Groups that have been stereotyped as less competent or hardworking often have to provide a larger, more compelling body of evidence to be judged as equally competent. Groups that have to "prove it again" include women, African Americans, Latinx people, individuals with disabilities, and Asian Americans.[59]

During the hiring process, this bias may mean that men who apply for managerial positions are evaluated based on their leadership potential, whereas women are judged on their past performance.[60] What does this look like in practice? "Before I'd hire her to lead a business unit, I'd want to make sure she's already been successful in that kind of role." For an equally qualified man, the comment might be: "Even though he hasn't led a business unit before, I just know he can do the job. He looks awesome."

Ways to combat personal bias during the interview process

Here are some ways to combat bias and avoid the "culture fit" trap:

- **Create objective criteria for reviewing resumes.**
  Choose the most critical requirements from the job description, and evaluate candidates on those qualities, not on their gender, age, favorite song, or other qualities that don't equate to being able to do the work.

- **Redact unnecessary personal information.**
  Resumes can include information that you don't need to evaluate and that might create bias, such as a candidate's name, schools attended, and home address.

Think about what you can strip from resumes or applications to reveal only what matters to your role.[61]

- **Use structured interview tactics.** Create interview questions focused on the skills and abilities your company is seeking. Ask each interviewee the same questions in the same order. (Don't make the same mistake as the team who interviewed my partner and me on the same day.)

- **Create a standardized scale or rubric for evaluating candidates**, and rank every interviewee on the same scale to help with decision making and eliminating "gut" feelings.[62]

- **Consider asking candidates to perform a work test**, assigning them a task that's similar to what they'd do if hired. Work tests are among the most reliable predictors of how someone will do in a job.[63]

- **Remind the interview team that bias can creep in.** Here's an approach that Google followed for removing bias from performance calibration sessions. In his book *Work Rules*, Laszlo Bock describes how at the start of Google's calibration meetings, everyone is given a simple handout describing common errors and biases that assessors make, and how to fix them.[64] Simply reminding managers of these biases was enough to eliminate many of them, and Google applied the same approach to interview teams. You can find their "unbiasing hiring" checklist online on their re:Work website.[65]

- **Restate the role and the experience you're looking for.** When the interview team meets to discuss candidates, get everyone on the same page. Remind them of the job requirements (ideally only five, as discussed in Chapter 3). You want to focus on the role and the candidate's experience, and avoid off-topic discussions of what someone liked or didn't like about a candidate, which might be based on bias.

- **Watch out for biased comments.** Here are some all-too-common phrases that should raise red flags during an interview debrief:

All-Too-Common Biased Comments

"That candidate doesn't have [some qualification that doesn't exist on the job description but that more privileged candidates meet]."

"They wouldn't want this role because of the travel."

"Before hiring them, I'd like to see them prove they can handle [responsibility they've already done]."

"I don't want to lower the bar."

"I'm not racist/sexist/homophobic, but [some comment about the candidate]."

"They wouldn't be a culture fit."

It's impossible to completely eliminate personal bias, but it's imperative to eliminate as much of it as possible.

Especially for those who are truly committed to hiring workers from marginalized groups.

Want to better recognize your personal bias? Take a free, online implicit association test on Harvard's Project Implicit website.[66]

Set up candidates for success

Ahead of the interview, send detailed information about the process and recommendations for how to prepare. Imagine you're their mentor, armed with insight into everything being discussed by the interview team. What would you share with them to help set them up for success during their interviews? Should they prepare a brief "elevator speech" about who they are and how their contributions have had an impact at their previous job? Should they wear a suit? Or should they NOT wear a suit because your workplace is very casual? If it's a video interview, can you arrange a trial run to ensure they have the right software and bandwidth? Is there a recent press release about your organization they should read?

I heard from one leader who decided to go a step further and provide all interview questions ahead of time. He wanted to ensure candidates on the autism spectrum would know what to expect and show up prepared and ready to do their best.

Microsoft also takes steps to attract candidates with autism and set them up for success. The company offers a practice interview with recruiters before doing the official one. They also allow candidates to do a coding assessment using their personal laptops instead of on a whiteboard in front of recruiters, which can be nerve-racking for anyone, but especially people with autism.[67]

If the candidate is coming on-site for an interview, provide information about physical accessibility, and ask if they need any accommodations. For example, include a map pointing out wheelchair access points. Ask if they'll need breaks to use a nursing mother's room (and if a fridge is available). Let them know you want them to be comfortable during their visit and that you want to know how you can best make that happen.

Speaking of on-site interviews, when they enter your workplace will candidates see photos displayed that reinforce your inclusive culture? I remember visiting Visa's San Francisco Innovation Center in 2019 and seeing walls of photos of employees from a recent Pride parade. Visa calls them a "diversity nudge" and believes they send a positive message to job seekers coming in for interviews.

Visa's photo display was in sharp contrast to what Rachel Maddow saw when visiting a university to hand out a prize for a prominent female scientist. She was overheard saying, "What is up with the dude wall?"[68]

We've all seen them. Walls covered with portraits of the male and pale who have made a significant contribution to their field or the institution. Maybe the founders of a company or prominent investors.

Do you have a "dude wall" at your office or institution? Think about the message it sends, to both candidates and existing employees. About who is valued. About who is bound for success. Then consider how you can redesign the wall to acknowledge and celebrate contributions by more than just white men.

Remember that "dude walls" aren't limited to framed oil paintings. They can be virtual. Like on the About page on your website.

Evaluate potential new hires on their inclusion experience

If you're trying to build a more inclusive environment, "it makes sense to stop letting in folks who would work against that goal," says diversity and inclusion consultant Jason Wong.[69] This means screening for inclusive attitudes and experiences during the interview process.

One simple way to do this is to ask candidates a question or two about their inclusion experience. Here are a few suggestions:

Inclusion Experience Interview Questions

"How have you contributed to an inclusive workplace culture or community?"

"Tell me about your experience working with diverse teams."

"What have you done to ensure coworkers feel a sense of belonging?"

"Have you had the opportunity to act as someone's ally at work? Tell me about it."

"If you were to take steps to diversify your team, what would you *not* do?"

By opening the door to this topic during the interview, I bet you'll be able to spot people who both talk the talk and walk the walk.

If you work in a male-dominated field like tech, consider this tip from open source evangelist Jan Wildeboer for eliminating candidates who exhibit a telling form of bias:

> *Heard of a cool tech-bro-weeding interview technique the other day. A male and female engineer conduct the interview session together. If, when the female engineer asks the candidate a question, he directs his answer to the male engineer, then he's out. They said it happens a lot.*[70]

Of course, your interview team should be prepared to answer questions from candidates about your organization's commitment to diversity and inclusion. Each person should also be ready to discuss how they participate in these efforts.

Pay attention to your interview team

When possible, make sure candidates meet at least one interviewer of their same gender, ethnicity, or age. By seeing someone "like them," candidates from underrepresented groups may feel more at ease and do better in the interview process. At Cisco, this practice resulted in a roughly 50 percent increase in the odds that a woman would be hired for a given position.[71]

That said, you don't want to burden employees from underrepresented demographics by asking them to do more interviewing than their peers. Being on an interview panel takes time away from the work that is going to be measured as part of quarterly or annual assessments. If you are tasking certain people with more than their fair share of interviewing, what can you do to reward them or set them up for success with the rest of their job responsibilities?

Lastly, make sure that all members of your interview panel have a real and respected voice in evaluating candidates. If you're inviting someone to be on your panel so that candidates can meet with someone "like them," their perspective should matter just as much as the rest of the panel.

Don't hold interviews in hotel bedrooms

At large professional conferences, organizations often hold interviews to tap into the students and other job seekers in attendance. Sounds great, except that due to a lack of meeting rooms, these interviews might take place in hotel bedrooms. Economics Ph.D. students Anna Stansbury and Kathryn Holston wrote a memo to call attention to the practice and why it's a problem. Not only can it be uncomfortable for anyone to have to sit on a bed for an interview, but women and LGBTQ people may face additional challenges. For sexual assault victims, it could be triggering. It could potentially put a candidate in a dangerous situation. Plus, there's stereotype threat; A woman going to an interview in a hotel bedroom may be concerned that someone will see her and wonder if she's sleeping her way to a job offer. As a result, she may not perform well during the interview.[72]

Find the leaks

If it looks like your company is not netting enough applicants from underrepresented groups, find out why. Evaluate your process, identify where these candidates drop out, and iterate. Use metrics from HR or your recruiting team to understand where the recruitment pipeline leaks happen. Is it during phone screens? Interviews? After the offer is made? Find out what's going wrong at which phase, and change that step.

For more ideas for being a better ally during the hiring process, check out the Leaky Tech Pipeline website from the Kapor Center for Social Impact.[73] The website's "Tech Workforce" section includes a "Featured Programs" subsection that connects the user to organizations that can help combat bias in interviewing, help companies find applicants from underrepresented groups, and shift workplace cultures.[74] Although it's a tech-specific site, many of the recommended tools can be used across industries.

Onboarding "diversity hires"

As you onboard new hires from underrepresented groups, consider that they might feel tokenized. They might believe that you hired them solely because you wanted a more diverse workforce, not because they were perfectly suited to the position. They might also be concerned that their new coworkers think the bar was lowered to make them an offer. They might hear someone say, "You're a diversity hire."

Here's a fantastic idea that Larissa Shapiro, a diversity and inclusion leader, shared with me:

> *Over our latest cohorts of interns, we have succeeded in massively changing the gender and ethnic diversity. And the students did seem to wonder if we had chosen them for their demographics, not their skills. I walked them through how we screen for interns, explaining how you only get through the (very) large initial pool by scoring well on our anonymized online code assessment, and that therefore the bar is no different for any of them. I explained how bias traditionally skews the selection process and how by blocking bias, we get the best talent, which is them. I could see the women and PoC [people of color] interns relax when we got through this. The screening is a firm and anonymized bar, and that helps.[75]*

Similarly, after software company Clio introduced a goal to hire more women, they made sure that every manager took the time to explain to new employees (regardless of gender) why they were hired and why Clio was excited they chose to accept their offer. They also made sure each woman who joined understood the company goal and how it worked, "instead of maybe hearing about it around the proverbial water cooler and creating her own narrative about it."[76]

Before wrapping up this section, I have one more tip: When hiring or promoting someone, be clear it's because they're the best person for the job. As Franklin Leonard, founder of The Black List, points out:

> *Don't tell people you hired or promoted someone because of their "diverse perspective." If that's part of it, then they got the job because they have a better understanding of your audience than the other candidates, which means they were the best candidate. Say that.*[77]
>
> *Saying you hired someone because of their "diverse perspective" is simply code for "I'm a good person because I hired someone that doesn't look like me" and simultaneously undervalues all the other contributions that person will make.*[78]

In other words, take the opportunity to set them up for success.

Checklist for Your Interview Process

☐ Create objective criteria for reviewing resumes.

☐ Redact unnecessary personal information from resumes.

☐ Use structured interview tactics and a rubric for evaluating candidates consistently.

☐ Ask candidates to perform a work test.

☐ Remind the interview team that bias can creep in.

☐ Restate the role and the requirements for the interview team.

☐ Set up candidates for success by sharing your interview process, tips for preparing for it, and asking about any accommodations they need.

☐ Evaluate candidates on how they've contributed to a diverse and inclusive workplace.

☐ Ensure the interview team can answer questions about the organizations' commitment to diversity and inclusion, and what they've done in support of these initiatives.

☐ When possible, ensure candidates meet at least one interviewer of their same gender, ethnicity, or age.

☐ Identify where people from underrepresented groups drop out of your hiring process and how you can stop these leaks.

☐ Tell new hires about your interview process and how it applies equally to everyone.

6

CONTINUE THE JOURNEY

Creating more inclusive hiring processes is an important step in diversifying a workforce, but alone it's not enough. Once you've hired people from underrepresented groups, you want to retain them and help them do their best work. You want to make sure that they feel included as valuable members of your team. That they feel they belong. That they can thrive.

In other words, you need to ensure your culture is inclusive.

I firmly believe that you don't have to be a manager or have the words "Diversity," "Inclusion," or "Belonging" on your business card to make a difference. There are everyday actions we all can take to create more inclusive workplaces. There are myriad ways we can be allies.

For ideas on how to level up your ally skills above and beyond the hiring process, check out my book, *Better Allies: Everyday Actions to Create Inclusive, Engaging Workplaces*. I wrote it to help anyone who cares about diversity but isn't sure what to do. Like this guidebook, it's packed full of stories, research, and straightforward steps to take.

I also have a weekly newsletter, "5 Ally Actions," where I share ideas curated from the week's news and my interactions with clients, audience members, and Twitter users from around the world. I'm on a mission myself to be a better ally, and I learn new approaches all the time. My goal is to share my learnings and to bring others along with me through this newsletter. You can subscribe at www.betterallies.com.

If you prefer social media, I'd love to have you follow @betterallies on Twitter, Instagram, Medium, or Pinterest.

Being an ally is a journey, and I hope you'll join me. Together, we can—and will—make a difference.

Continue the Journey

Read *Better Allies: Everyday Actions to Create Inclusive, Engaging Workplaces.*

Subscribe to the "5 Ally Actions" weekly newsletter at www.betterallies.com.

Follow @betterallies on Twitter, Instagram, Medium, or Pinterest.

RECAP: HIRING CHECKLISTS

Here's a compilation of the checklists from each chapter.

Checklist for Your Careers Page

☐ Explore the photos on your company's careers page. What message do they send to candidates? Do they show real employees, representing the true diversity within your company? Do they have captions or HTML alt tags for people using screen readers?

☐ Review how you describe the culture of your company. Do you list employee resource groups and other offerings that demonstrate a commitment to an inclusive workplace?

☐ Look at how you describe the kinds of candidates you're looking for. Are there changes to make to be more inclusive of people of different genders, ethnicities, religions, sexual orientations, ages, and abilities? Can you be actively inclusive of candidates who have spent time unemployed? Do you welcome veterans? Do you encourage people to apply even if they don't meet 100 percent of the requirements?

☐ Are you transparent about your interview process?

☐ Think about how your company or customers contribute to social good. Is this explained clearly on your careers page?

☐ Do you emphasize employee benefits, especially those important to caregivers?

Checklist for Your Job Descriptions

☐ Can you find any biased language? E.g., Words that imply the candidate is a certain gender or from a particular background. "Man" words ("right-hand man," "superman," etc). Or other masculine-coded words like "aggressive," "competitive," and "assertive." Or sports terminology. How would you edit it to be less biased?

☐ Drop "preferred" requirements, degrees, and certifications (unless truly needed).

☐ Combine similar or duplicate requirements to simplify the description.

☐ Remove skills that can easily be taught on the job.

☐ For managerial positions, do you require prior experience leading diverse teams? If not, consider adding it to attract candidates who value diversity.

☐ For technical roles, do you require open source experience? Or a candidate's GitHub profile? Unless it's truly required, remove it.

☐ For everything else: ask, "If an otherwise perfect candidate came along without this experience, would we still hire them?" If so, cut it. Aim for a maximum of five requirements.

Checklist for Your Candidate Pool

☐ Identify where you advertise your job openings. If it tends to be only one or two job sites, think about how you could cast a wider net.

☐ Are you tapping your current workforce to recommend candidates from underrepresented groups? Do you offer an incentive for referring them? Do you hold sourcing parties to get more referrals? Do you keep your employees informed about the status of their referrals?

☐ Most of us have homogeneous networks, which lead to hiring homogeneity. Think about your network and steps you can take to diversify it before you need to hire from it.

☐ Do you encourage current employees from underrepresented groups to be visible externally? Can you do more to support them?

☐ Do you have a mandate or quota for interviewing people from underrepresented groups?

☐ Are you open to candidates who haven't had the expected journey of highly-selective universities, internships, name-brand company experience, etc?

Checklist for Your Interview Process

☐ Create objective criteria for reviewing resumes.

☐ Redact unnecessary personal information from resumes.

☐ Use structured interview tactics and a rubric for evaluating candidates consistently.

☐ Ask candidates to perform a work test.

☐ Remind the interview team that bias can creep in.

☐ Restate the role and the requirements for the interview team.

☐ Set up candidates for success by sharing your interview process, tips for preparing for it, and asking about any accommodations they need.

☐ Evaluate candidates on how they've contributed to a diverse and inclusive workplace.

☐ Ensure the interview team can answer questions about the organizations' commitment to diversity and inclusion, and what they've done in support of these initiatives.

☐ When possible, ensure candidates meet at least one interviewer of their same gender, ethnicity, or age.

☐ Identify where people from underrepresented groups drop out of your hiring process and how you can stop these leaks.

☐ Tell new hires about your interview process and how it applies equally to everyone.

GRATITUDE

This guidebook was born from a chapter in my previous book, *Better Allies: Everyday Actions to Create Inclusive, Engaging Workplaces*. When my friend Joe Dunn read *Better Allies*, he casually mentioned that the chapter on hiring could be an entire book. I took that as a challenge. Thank you, Joe, for seeding the idea and for reading an advanced copy.

I also want to thank my editor, Sally McGraw, and my beta readers who were gracious with their time and provided me with outstanding feedback. To Marcia Dority Baker, Bev Carleton, Patrick Chan, Caroline Chavier, Martijn Grooten, Alastair Hill, Emma Jackson, Kyle Johnson, Shawn McCarthy, Colleen McCreary, Julia McMillan, Sarah Mei, Thuy Le, Kristen Pressner, Bobbie Riley, and Arti Sharma, I'm so very grateful.

Last but not least, hugs and thanks to my partner Tim and our children Emma and Ted. You reviewed many drafts and helped me through the painstaking process of honing in on the right cover design. (I still don't understand why I find that to be the hardest part of publishing a book.) Your encouragement and support make me a better version of myself.

ABOUT THE AUTHOR

Karen Catlin is a passionate advocate for inclusion in the workplace. After spending twenty-five years building software products and serving as a vice president of engineering at Macromedia and Adobe, she witnessed a sharp decline in the number of women working in tech. Frustrated but galvanized, she knew it was time to switch gears.

Today, Karen is a leadership coach, keynote speaker, and author. She's a highly sought-after and engaging presenter who has delivered talks at hundreds of events. In addition to speaking herself, Karen is determined to bring more diversity to speaker lineups at tech industry events. To support this goal, she coauthored *Present! A Techie's Guide to Public Speaking* with Poornima Vijayashanker.

In 2014, Karen started the Twitter handle @betterallies to share simple, actionable steps that anyone could take to make their workplace more inclusive. That Twitter handle became the inspiration for her books, *Better Allies: Everyday Actions to Create Inclusive, Engaging Workplaces* and *The Better Allies™ Approach to Hiring*. She continues to tweet and blog for Better Allies and emails a roundup of "5 Ally Actions" to her subscribers every week.

Karen is a graduate and active alum of Brown University, serving as an advisor to the university's Computer Science Diversity Initiative and mentoring students on how to launch their careers. She's also on the advisory boards for the Women's CLUB of Silicon Valley and WEST (Women Entering and Staying in Technology). In 2015, the California State Assembly honored Karen with the Wonder Women Tech Innovator Award for outstanding achievements in business and technology and for being a role model for women.

Karen and her partner Tim live in San Mateo, California. They're the proud parents of two Gen Z children, Emma and Ted.

To find out what Karen's up to next or invite her to speak at your next event, visit her website at www.karencatlin.com.

NOTES

Introduction

1   "Why Gender Diversity May Lead to Better Returns for Investors," Morgan Stanley, March 7, 2019, https://www.morganstanley.com/access/gender-diversity.

2   Laszlo Bock, "Your employment engagement survey is destroying your company's culture," *Fast Company*, April 22, 2019, https://www.fastcompany.com/90335847/your-engagement-survey-is-destroying-your-companys-culture.

Chapter 1

3   Sohan Murthy, "Measuring Gender Diversity with Data from LinkedIn," *LinkedIn Official Blog*, June 17, 2015, https://blog.linkedin.com/2015/06/17/measuring-gender-diversity-with-data-from-linkedin.

4   Joelle Emerson, "Want to Hire More a More Diverse Set of People? Raise Your Bar." *Medium*, May 11, 2015, https://medium.com/inclusion-insights/want-to-hire-more-diverse-people-raise-your-bar-b5d30f91cbd9.

5   Jessi Hempel, "Why Are There Few Women in Tech? Watch a Recruiting Session," *Wired*, March 1, 2018, https://www.wired.com/story/why-are-there-few-women-in-tech-watch-a-recruiting-session/.

6   Makinde Adeagbo, "Racial Fault Lines in Silicon Valley," *Medium*, May 25, 2016, https://blog.devcolor.org/racial-fault-lines-in-silicon-valley-390cd0e4a6dc.

7   Lesley Evans Ogden, "Working mothers face a 'wall' of bias—but there are ways to push back," *Science*, April 10, 2019, https://www.sciencemag.org/careers/2019/04/working-mothers-face-wall-bias-there-are-ways-push-back.

8   Jena McGregor, "Lawmakers to introduce first federal bills to ban race-based hair discrimination," *Washington Post,* December 5, 2019, https://www.washingtonpost.com/business/2019/12/05/lawmakers-introduce-first-federal-bills-ban-race-based-hair-discrimination/.

Chapter 2

9   "Top 10 Ways to Hire the Best for Your Computing Start-Up," National Center for Women in Information Technology, accessed September 29, 2018, https://www.ncwit.org/resources/top-10-ways-hire-best-your-computing-start/top-10-ways-hire-best-your-computing-start.

10   Better Allies (@betterallies), "I use photos of actual employees on my careers page. To be genuine and authentic. Unlike Dow, who uses a stock photo of a "happy african american worker." https://corporate.dow.com/en-us/careers #BetterAllies #RepresentationMatters #Inclusion," Twitter, September 5, 2019, 1:08 p.m., https://twitter.com/betterallies/status/1169703873012912128.

11   Entertainment Software Association, *2014 Essential Facts about the Computer and Video Game Industry*, 2014, http://www.theesa.com/wp-content/uploads/2014/10/ESA_EF_2014.pdf; Audrey L. Brehm, "Navigating the Feminine in Massively Multiplayer Online Games: Gender in World of Warcraft," *Frontiers in Psychology* 4 (2013): 903, https://doi.org/10.3389/fpsyg.2013.00903.

12   Zapier Jobs page, accessed September 3, 2019, https://zapier.com/jobs/.

13   MIT employee resource groups page, accessed September 5, 2019, https://hr.mit.edu/diversity-inclusion/ergs.

14   Change.org post on its LinkedIn page, July 2019, https://www.linkedin.com/posts/change-org_changeorg-is-committed-to-diversity-and-activity-6562451509731225600-ddNt.

15   Republic Services, "Hiring our Heroes," accessed September 13, 2019, https://republicservices-veterans.jobs/.

16   Original study unavailable. See summaries in: Sheryl Sandberg, *Lean In: Women, Work, and the Will to Lead*, with Nell Scovell (New York: Alfred A. Knopf, 2013); Katty Kay and Claire Shipman, *The Confidence Code: The Science and Art of Self-Assurance—What Women Should Know* (New York: HarperCollins, 2014).

17   Jo Owen, *How to Lead* (Upper Saddle River, NJ: Prentice Hall, 2011).

18   Tara Sophia Mohr, "Why Women Don't Apply for Jobs Unless
     They're 100% Qualified," *Harvard Business Review*, August 25, 2014,
     https://hbr.org/2014/08/why-women-dont-apply-for-jobs-unless-
     theyre-100-qualified.

19   Webflow job description, accessed August 24, 2019,
     https://webflow.com/jobs?gh_jid=1812891.

20   Anne McCarthy, "Trust, Growth, Inclusion: A Study of Women
     Engineers' Job-Search Priorities," *Automattic Blog*, September 4, 2019,
     https://en-blog.files.wordpress.com/2019/08/trust-growth-
     inclusion-e28093-a-study-of-women-engineerse28099-job-search-
     priorities.pdf.

21   Automattic, "How We Hire Developers," accessed August 29, 2019,
     https://automattic.com/work-with-us/how-we-hire-developers/.

22   P&G, "Our Hiring Process," accessed September 5, 2019,
     https://www.pgcareers.com/hiring-process.

23   Adobe, "Our core values," accessed October 22, 2019,
     https://www.adobe.com/about-adobe/fast-facts.html#values.

24   Oliver Staley, "Uber has replaced Travis Kalanick's values with eight
     new 'cultural norms'," *Quartz*, November 7, 2017,
     https://qz.com/work/1123038/uber-has-replaced-travis-kalanicks-
     values-with-eight-new-cultural-norms/.

25   Clifton Leaf, "Salesforce Founder Marc Benioff: What Business
     School Never Taught Me," *Fortune*, October 15, 2019,
     https://fortune.com/longform/marc-benioff-billionaire-business-
     advice-salesforce.

26   Life at Visa, accessed October 13, 2019, https://usa.visa.com/about-
     visa/diversity-inclusion/life-at-visa.html.

27   Cate Huston, "Sharing the Data: How Technical Women Navigate
     Their Career," *Wordpress Developer Blog*, August 28, 2019,
     https://developer.wordpress.com/2019/08/28/sharing-the-data-
     how-technical-women-navigate-their-career/.

28   "Who Are the Caregivers?" Family Caregiving Alliance, December
     31, 2003, https://www.caregiver.org/women-and-caregiving-facts-
     and-figures.

Chapter 3

29   "Supervising-in-a-Box Series: Employee Recruitment/Selection,"
     National Center for Women in Information Technology, February
     12, 2010, https://www.ncwit.org/resources/supervising-box-series-
     employee-recruitmentselection.

30   Danielle Gaucher, Justin Friesen, and Aaron C. Kay, "Evidence That
     Gendered Wording in Job Advertisements Exists and Sustains
     Gender Inequality," *Journal of Personality and Social Psychology* 101, no. 1
     (July 2011): 109–28, https://doi.org/10.1037/a0022530.

31   Diversity Dialogs (@Diverse_Dialogs), "Even in this day and age,
     jobs are being advertised for 'men only'. Saddening." Twitter, April
     28, 2019, 10:22 a.m.,
     https://twitter.com/Diverse_Dialogs/status/1122551700127006720.

32   Jason Anderson (@dirkgently), "They also have this lovely opening
     for the Females Only quota." Twitter, April 28, 2019, 6:28 p.m.,
     https://twitter.com/dirkgently/status/1122674096091934720.

33   Helena (@misshelenasue), "Uh, hey @cynetjobs - what's with this?
     Your job listing for a mid-senior level business development
     position's top qualification is 'Preferably Caucasian' How could you
     POSSIBLY think that's okay?" Twitter, April 26, 2019, 11:18 p.m.,
     https://twitter.com/misshelenasue/status/1122022082404081670.

34   Tech Companies That Only Hire Men (website), accessed August 18,
     2018, http://techcompaniesthatonlyhiremen.tumblr.com/.

35   Courtney Connley, "Google, Apple and 12 other companies that no
     longer require employees to have a college degree," *CNBC*, October
     8, 2018, https://www.cnbc.com/2018/08/16/15-companies-that-
     no-longer-require-employees-to-have-a-college-degree.html.

36   Klint Finley, "Diversity in Open Source Is Even Worse Than in Tech
     Overall," *Wired*, June 2, 2017,
     https://www.wired.com/2017/06/diversity-open-source-even-
     worse-tech-overall/.

37   Lori Mackenzie, Alison Wynn, and Shelley Correll, "If Women Don't
     Apply to Your Company, This Is Probably Why," October 17, 2019,
     Harvard Business Review, https://hbr.org/2019/10/if-women-dont-
     apply-to-your-company-this-is-probably-why.

Chapter 4

38 Allison Scott, Freada Kapor Klein, Frieda McAlear, Alexis Martin, and Sonia Koshy, *The Leaky Tech Pipeline: A Comprehensive Framework for Understanding and Addressing the Lack of Diversity across the Tech Ecosystem* (Oakland, CA: Kapor Center for Social Impact, February 2018), http://www.leakytechpipeline.com/wp-content/themes/kapor/pdf/KC18001_report_v6.pdf.

39 Rachel Thomas, Marianne Cooper, Ellen Konar, Megan Rooney, Ashley Finch, Lareina Yee, Alexis Krivkovich, Irina Starikova, Kelsey Robinson, and Rachel Valentino, *Women in the Workplace 2017* (New York and Palo Alto, CA: McKinsey & Company and LeanIn.Org, 2017), https://womenintheworkplace.com/2017.

40 Devon Magliozzi, "Building Effective Networks: Nurturing Strategic Relationships, Especially for Women," The Clayman Institute for Gender Research, April 26, 2016, https://gender.stanford.edu/news-publications/gender-news/building-effective-networks-nurturing-strategic-relationships.

41 Drake Baer, "Why You Need a Diverse Network," August 13, 2013, *Fast Company*, https://www.fastcompany.com/3015552/why-you-need-a-diverse-network.

42 Samantha Geitz (@SamanthaGeitz), "You have to build a network for diversity. This takes YEARS. I want to write another thread or maybe blog on how to do this, but I'll tell you how you can start today. Follow 10 people on Twitter who aren't white dudes. Chat with them every so often. Do it without an agenda." Twitter, August 29, 2019, 6:24 a.m., https://twitter.com/SamanthaGeitz/status/1167065417317306368.

43 Kendall Tucker, "Tips for Hiring Women in Tech from a Female Ceo Who Had Trouble Hiring Women in Tech," *W2.0*, July 17, 2018, http://www.women2.com/2018/07/17/tips-for-hiring-women-in-tech-from-a-female-ceo-who-had-trouble-hiring-women-in-tech/.

44 Stack Overflow Developer Survey Results 2019, accessed August 28, 2019, https://insights.stackoverflow.com/survey/2019#developer-profile-_-gender.

45   Cate Huston, "Sharing the Data: How Technical Women Navigate Their Career," *Wordpress Developer Blog*, August 28, 2019, https://developer.wordpress.com/2019/08/28/sharing-the-data-how-technical-women-navigate-their-career/.

46   Abby Maldonado, "Diversifying Engineering Referrals at Pinterest," *LinkedIn*, January 15, 2016, https://www.linkedin.com/pulse/diversifying-engineering-referrals-pinterest-abby-maldonado/.

47   Dawn Onley, "Sourcing Parties Vest Employees in the Recruitment Process," *Society for Human Resource Management*, June 8, 2018, https://www.shrm.org/resourcesandtools/hr-topics/talent-acquisition/pages/sourcing-parties-vest-employees-recruitment-process.aspx.

48   Kenneth Johnson, "What Corporations Can Learn about Diversity from the NFL's Rooney Rule," *Forbes*, February 1, 2018, https://www.forbes.com/sites/forbescoachescouncil/2018/02/01/what-corporations-can-learn-about-diversity-from-the-nfls-rooney-rule/#360cd19347de.

49   Jethro Nededog, "J.J. Abrams Believes Diversity Is Good for Business—and He's Taking One Big Step to Prove It," *Business Insider*, March 2, 2016, https://www.businessinsider.com/jj-abrams-diversity-policy-2016-3.

50   Christina Passariello, "Tech Firms Borrow Football Play to Increase Hiring of Women," *Wall Street Journal*, September 27, 2016, https://www.wsj.com/articles/tech-firms-borrow-football-play-to-increase-hiring-of-women-1474963562.

51   Maitane Sardon and Dieter Holger, "What's Holding Companies Back From Expanding Diversity," *Wall Street Journal*, October 26, 2019, https://www.wsj.com/articles/whats-holding-companies-back-from-expanding-diversity-11572091206.

52   Stefanie K. Johnson, "What Amazon's Board Was Getting Wrong About Diversity and Hiring," *Harvard Business Review*, May 14, 2018, https://hbr.org/2018/05/what-amazons-board-is-getting-wrong-about-diversity-and-hiring.

53   Minda Harts, *The Memo* (Seal Press, 2019).

Chapter 5

54 "Tech Workforce Barriers," Kapor Center for Social Impact, accessed November 1, 2018, http://www.leakytechpipeline.com/barrier/tech-workforce-barriers/.

55 Lauren A. Rivera, "Guess Who Doesn't Fit In at Work," *New York Times*, May 30, 2015, https://www.nytimes.com/2015/05/31/opinion/sunday/guess-who-doesnt-fit-in-at-work.html.

56 Sue Shellenbarger, "The Dangers of Hiring for Cultural Fit," *Wall Street Journal*, September 23, 2019, https://www.wsj.com/articles/the-dangers-of-hiring-for-cultural-fit-11569231000.

57 Textio, "Webinar: How to Fight Diversity Fatigue," Vimeo video, May 14, 2018, 56:24, https://vimeo.com/269693446/624660f941.

58 Lydia Dishman, "How Google, Pinterest, and Others Use Internships to Push Their Diversity Initiatives," *Fast Company*, May 23, 2016, https://www.fastcompany.com/3060118/how-google-pinterest-and-others-use-internships-to-push-their-diversity-i.

59 "Interrupting Bias in Performance Evaluations," Bias Interrupters, accessed November 1, 2018, https://biasinterrupters.org/interrupting-bias-in-performance-evaluations/.

60 Abigail Player, Georgina Randsley de Moura, Ana C. Leite, Dominic Abrams, and Fatima Tresh, "Overlooked Leadership Potential: The Preference for Leadership Potential in Job Candidates Who Are Men vs. Women," *Frontiers in Psychology*, April 16, 2019, https://www.frontiersin.org/articles/10.3389/fpsyg.2019.00755/full.

61 Michael Grothaus, "How "Blind Recruitment" Works And Why You Should Consider It," *Fast Company*, March 14, 2016, https://www.fastcompany.com/3057631/how-blind-recruitment-works-and-why-you-should-consider.

62 Iris Bohnet, "How to Take the Bias out of Interviews," *Harvard Business Review*, April 18, 2016, https://hbr.org/2016/04/how-to-take-the-bias-out-of-interviews.

63   Laszlo Bock, "Here's Google's Secret to Hiring the Best People,"
     Wired, April 7, 2015, https://www.wired.com/2015/04/hire-like-
     google/.

64   Laszlo Bock, *Work Rules! Insights from Inside Google That Will Transform
     How You Live and Lead* (New York: Twelve Books, 2015).

65   re:Work (website), "Google's unbiasing hiring checklists," accessed
     August 27, 2019,
     https://docs.google.com/document/d/1_1qvG7ESd2kJj7QJKsUO
     bwMJShswvzurNmpmbM7LE3Y/export?format=pdf.

66   Project Implicit (website), accessed November 1, 2018,
     https://implicit.harvard.edu.

67   Maitane Sardon, "How Microsoft Tapped the Autism Community
     for Talent," *Wall Street Journal*, October 26, 2019,
     https://www.wsj.com/articles/how-microsoft-tapped-the-autism-
     community-for-talent-11572091210.

68   Nell Greenfieldboyce, "Academic Science Rethinks All-Too-White
     'Dude Walls' Of Honor," *NPR*, August 25, 2019,
     https://www.npr.org/sections/health-
     shots/2019/08/25/749886989/academic-science-rethinks-all-too-
     white-dude-walls-of-honor.

69   Jason Wong, "Inclusion Interviewing," *Jason Wong's Blog*, July 2, 2018,
     https://www.attack-gecko.net/2018/07/02/inclusion-interviewing/.

70   Jan Wildeboer (@jwildeboer), "Heard of a cool tech-bro-weeding
     interview technique the other day. A male and female engineer
     conduct the interview session together. If, when the female engineer
     asks the candidate a question, he directs his answer to the male
     engineer, then he's out. They said it happens a lot" Twitter, August
     29, 2019, 3:57 a.m.,
     https://twitter.com/jwildeboer/status/1167028431059599360.

71   Lindsay Gellman and Georgia Wells, "What's Holding Back Women
     in Tech?" *Wall Street Journal*, March 22, 2016,
     https://www.wsj.com/articles/whats-holding-back-women-in-tech-
     1458639004.

72 Sean McHenry and Kai Ryssdal, "Economists want to end hotel room job interviews," *Marketplace*, September 4, 2019, https://www.marketplace.org/2019/09/04/economists-want-to-end-hotel-room-job-interviews/.

73 The Leaky Tech Pipeline (website), Kapor Center for Social Impact, http://www.leakytechpipeline.com/.

74 "Programs & Initiatives," The Leaky Tech Pipeline, accessed November 1, 2018, http://www.leakytechpipeline.com/featured-programs/tech-workforce/.

75 Larissa Shapiro, personal communication, September 20, 2018.

76 Ainsley Robertson, "How we doubled the representation of women in Engineering at Clio," *Clio Labs blog*, August 28, 2019, https://labs.clio.com/how-we-doubled-the-representation-of-women-in-engineering-at-clio-2d9a4a1a0282.

77 Franklin Leonard (@franklinleonard), "Don't tell people you hired or promoted someone because of their 'diverse perspective.' If that's part of it, then they got the job because they have a better understanding of your audience than the other candidates, which means they were the best candidate. Say that." Twitter, November 22, 2019, 6:38 p.m., https://twitter.com/franklinleonard/status/1198068279144669185.

78 Franklin Leonard (@franklinleonard), "Saying you hired someone because of their "diverse perspective" is simply code for "I'm a good person because I hired someone that doesn't look like me" and simultaneously undervalues all the other contributions that person will make." Twitter, November 22, 2019, 6:43 p.m., https://twitter.com/franklinleonard/status/1198069650816303104.